STAYING

Financial freedom for spouses
Building a sustainable life together

YOUNG

STAYING

Financial freedom for spouses
Building a sustainable life together

YOUNG

Kiran Dange, M.D.

Kanchan Bala Rathore, M.S.

Bigfoot Publications
Because, there's a writer in everyone.

Staying Young: Financial Freedom for Spouses (Building a Sustainable Life Together)
Author: Kiran Dange, M.D., Kanchan Bala Rathore, M.S.

First Published by
Bigfoot06 Publications (OPC) Pvt. Ltd.
1st floor, BSR Building near Vishal Mega Mart,Daultabad Flyover, Laxman Vihar Phase 3, Gurugram, Haryana (122001)
Website: www.bigfootpublications.in
Email: info@bigfootpublications.in

First Edition: April, 2024

ISBN Print Book: 978-81-970347-2-5

Typeset in Garamond 12pt
by Yachika Prajapati For Bigfoot06 Publications,

Printed in India

Dedicated To

Aashima and Ashmayu: Dedicated to my beloved children, the spark of my imagination, and the joy in my tale.

Dr. Ravindra and Dr. Nirupama: Dedicated to my respected siblings, my lifelong co-authors of adventure and guidance.

Dr. Kanchan: Dedicated to my dear spouse, my steadfast critique, and my strong support system in the narrative of life.

Shri. Jagannathji and Shrimati. Suryakantaji: "Dedicated to my respected parents, the authors of my beginning, the inspiration for my legacy, and the humble foundation upon which my story is built.

PREFACE

Picture the Saas-Bahu saga taking a backseat as couples unite to decode the Da Vinci code of Indian Family and provide the just means to be happy not only with themselves but also for their parents, in-laws, and children! It's not just about keeping up with the Patels anymore; it's about out-investing them! In this financial 'Nagin Dance,' every move is synchronized to the beat of mutual funds, stocks, and real estate. It's a fiscal fiesta where 'his' and 'her' become 'ours,' and the only thing that's separate is the tax benefits. And let's not forget the in-laws, who now double as unofficial financial advisors, adding their two rupees to every financial decision.

In a land where the currency of love is as rich as its spices, our spirited spouses are cooking up a storm in the kitchen of commerce. They're blending budgets like they're mixing masalas, creating a recipe for economic ecstasy that's as flavorful as it is fiscally fabulous. With a sparkle in their eyes and calculators in their hands, these financial freedom fighters are embarking on a thrilling safari through the jungle of investments, navigating the terrain with the ease of tiger trackers. They've got their mutual funds on the prowl and their stocks soaring like eagles. These partners in prosperity aren't just crossing bridges; they're building them out of solid gold savings and bonds of trust. They're turning the game of life into a two-player co-op mission, where every level up is a step closer to that penthouse of plenty. Watch as they lock arms and skip down the yellow brick road of responsible risk-taking, singing in harmony with the chorus of compound interest.

They're not just dreaming of a future; they're drafting it with the precision of architects, designing a palace of prosperity where every brick is a shared goal achieved.

In today's masala mix of modern Indian marriages, financial planning is the new love language. Forget whispering sweet noting's; it's sexier to discuss asset allocation over a candle-lit dinner. And when it comes to spending, think of it as a Bollywood dance-off – synchronized, dramatic, but always on beat. So, gear up for a joint adventure in the land of ledger books and love. With a pinch of humor, a dash of strategy, and a whole lot of mutual respect, financial freedom is the new 'happily ever after.' After all, when it comes to money matters, two heads (and wallets) are better than one!

ACKNOWLEDGMENTS

First and foremost, I extend my heartfelt thanks to my alma mater, whose rigorous academic environment and supportive community laid the foundation for my passion for lifelong learning and personal growth. The lessons learned and friendships forged there have been invaluable.

A special note of appreciation goes to my circle of friends, colleagues and students in the medical field. Your insights, encouragement, and the shared experiences have been instrumental in shaping my approach to holistic wellness and financial health. To the common man whose stories of resilience, love, and partnership have been the true inspiration behind this work, I am deeply grateful. Your journeys have underscored the importance of financial freedom in living a fulfilled life together.

I cannot express enough gratitude to Bigfoot Publishing House for believing in this project. A special gratitude to my editor, whose keen eye and thoughtful suggestions have greatly enhanced the clarity and impact of this manuscript. Your guidance has been a beacon throughout this process. To the incredibly talented content designer, who brought the vision for the cover and back page to life with creativity and passion, thank you. Your artistry has given this book an inviting gateway. My appreciation also extends to the skilled typesetter and printers whose meticulous attention to formatting has provided this book with the professional and accessible presentation it deserves. Your expertise has ensured that our content is not only readable but also visually engaging.

This book is a testament to the power of collaboration, support, and shared vision. To everyone who has been a part of this journey, thank you. Together, we have created a resource that I hope will inspire and guide couples toward a future of financial freedom and enduring youthfulness.

Contents

CHAPTER 1

INTRODUCTION TO FINANCIAL FREEDOM FOR SPOUSES

Understanding the Importance of Financial Freedom in a Relationship

In any relationship, financial freedom plays a crucial role in ensuring a sustainable and harmonious life together. This introductory paragraph sheds light on the significance of attaining financial independence as a couple and how it can positively impact various aspects of life, from aesthetics to a sustainable lifestyle.

For spouses, financial freedom means having the ability to make choices without being restricted by monetary constraints. It allows individuals to pursue their passions, invest in personal growth, and contribute to the overall well-being of the relationship. When both partners are financially independent, they can share responsibilities and make decisions together, creating a sense of equality and mutual respect.

Professionals and students can benefit greatly from understanding the importance of financial freedom in relationships. By establishing a solid financial foundation, they can focus on their careers or studies without the added stress of financial instability. Picture a world where professionals are free to pursue their passions, unhindered by financial limitations. Imagine the creativity and innovation that could flourish if individuals were not held back by financial concerns. With financial freedom, this dream becomes a reality, allowing individuals to choose fulfilling careers that bring them joy and purpose.

Consumerism plays a significant role in modern society, often leading to unsustainable spending habits. Understanding the importance of financial freedom can help individuals break free from the cycle of mindless consumption and embrace a more sustainable lifestyle. By prioritizing financial independence, couples can make informed decisions about their purchases, investing in experiences and products that align with their values and contribute to a more sustainable future.

Financial independence is not solely about accumulating wealth; it is about having control over one's financial destiny. By understanding the importance of financial freedom, individuals can develop healthy financial habits and strive for long-term financial security. This sub-chapter will provide practical tips and strategies for achieving financial independence, such as budgeting, saving, and investing wisely.

Ultimately, financial freedom in a relationship empowers couples to lead fulfilling lives, both individually and together. It promotes open communication about money matters, reduces stress and conflict, and fosters an environment of trust and collaboration. By embracing the concepts of aesthetics, life, money, and sustainable living, couples can embark on a journey toward financial freedom and build a sustainable life together.

Benefits of Building a Sustainable Life Together

In today's fast-paced world, building a sustainable life together as spouses has become more important than ever. Not only does it contribute to a healthier environment, but it also brings numerous benefits to our personal well-being, finances, and relationships.

One of the key benefits of adopting a sustainable lifestyle is the positive impact it has on the environment. By adopting eco-friendly practices and reducing our carbon footprint, we help preserve our planet for future generations. This not only helps combat climate change but also fosters a sense of responsibility and purpose within our relationship.

Furthermore, building a sustainable life together can significantly improve our financial situation. Sustainable choices such as energy-efficient appliances, water-saving techniques, and mindful consumption can lead to substantial cost savings over time. By reducing our reliance on wasteful products and services, we can redirect those saved funds towards investments, savings, or experiences that truly matter to us as a couple.

A sustainable lifestyle also promotes a healthier and more fulfilling life. By prioritizing physical and mental well-being, we can reduce stress levels and improve overall quality of life. Engaging in activities such as hiking, cycling, or gardening not only helps us stay active but also strengthens our bond as a couple. Additionally, adopting a plant-based diet or supporting local farmers promotes better nutrition and supports local economies.

Embracing sustainability as a couple also fosters stronger relationships. It provides opportunities for shared goals, values, and experiences, which strengthens the bond between partners. Collaborating on sustainable projects, such as building a composting system or starting a community garden, encourages teamwork and communication. This sense of shared purpose and accomplishment can enhance trust, respect, and mutual understanding within the relationship.

Finally, a sustainable lifestyle sets an excellent example for others – be it friends, family, or the wider community. By demonstrating our commitment to living a life that balances aesthetics, life, and money, we inspire others to follow suit.

Our actions can create a ripple effect, leading to a more sustainable and responsible society as a whole.

In conclusion, building a sustainable life together offers numerous benefits for spouses. It not only contributes to the preservation of our environment but also leads to financial freedom, improved well-being, stronger relationships, and the ability to inspire others. By embracing sustainability as a couple, we can create a more fulfilling and purposeful life for ourselves and future generations.

CHAPTER 2

AESTHETICS, LIFE, AND MONEY

Exploring the Relationship Between Aesthetics and Financial Freedom: Indian Philosophy vis a vis Western Philosophy

In today's fast-paced world, the pursuit of financial freedom has become a primary goal for many individuals. However, in the race to accumulate wealth, the importance of aesthetics and its connection to a sustainable lifestyle often gets overlooked. This subdivision aims to shed light on the relationship between aesthetics and financial freedom, drawing insights from both Indian and Western philosophies.

Indian philosophy, deeply rooted in spirituality and mindfulness, offers a unique perspective on the interplay between aesthetics and financial freedom. It emphasizes the concept of "Dharma" or balance, encouraging individuals to find harmony in all aspects of life, including their finances. By adopting a sustainable and conscious approach to money management, one can align their financial goals with their personal values, leading to a more fulfilling and aesthetically pleasing life.

Western philosophy, on the other hand, tends to place a greater emphasis on material wealth and external validation. However, recent trends in sustainable living and minimalism have started to challenge these conventional notions. By embracing a minimalist lifestyle and focusing on experiences rather than material possessions, individuals can find financial freedom without compromising their aesthetic preferences.

Realizing the link between aesthetics and financial freedom can be truly transformative. With a focus on a sustainable lifestyle and financial independence, individuals can pave the way for a more fulfilling and meaningful existence. This bit delves into practical strategies for integrating aesthetics and financial freedom into everyday life. It will explore the concept of conscious consumerism, encouraging individuals to make mindful choices that align with their values. Additionally, it will provide tips on budgeting and saving, emphasizing the importance of striking a balance between financial stability and pursuing aesthetic pleasures.

Ultimately, by exploring the relationship between aesthetics and financial freedom, readers will gain valuable insights into how to build a sustainable life together. Whether you are a spouse looking to align your financial goals with your aesthetic preferences or a student seeking a more conscious approach to money management, this part of the chapter will provide practical advice and thought-provoking ideas to help you achieve a sustainable lifestyle and financial independence.

Join us on this journey as we explore the fascinating connection between aesthetics, life, and money, and discover the path to a more fulfilling and aesthetically pleasing existence.

Understanding How Lifestyle Choices Impact Financial Independence

In today's fast-paced world, it is essential to be mindful of how our lifestyle choices can impact our financial independence. Whether you are a multisphere engager or any part of society, understanding the correlation between your lifestyle and financial well-being is crucial for building a sustainable life together. It discusses how our choices in aesthetics, life, and money, and adopting a sustainable lifestyle can greatly influence our journey towards financial freedom.

Aesthetics play a significant role in our lives. From fashion to home decor, our aesthetic choices often come with a price tag. However, it is important to strike a balance between expressing our style and being financially responsible. By being mindful of our spending habits and opting for quality over quantity, we can make informed decisions that align with our financial goals. Here we will delve into the importance of budgeting for aesthetic choices and how it can contribute to long-term financial independence.

Life and money are intertwined in more ways than we realize. Our lifestyle choices, such as the activities we engage in and the experiences we seek, can have a significant impact on our financial well-being. By consciously evaluating our priorities and aligning them with our financial goals, we can make informed choices that support our journey toward financial independence. We will explore various aspects of life, such as travel, hobbies, and entertainment, and how they can be enjoyed without compromising our financial stability.

Adopting a sustainable lifestyle not only benefits the environment but also plays a crucial role in our financial independence. We can save money in the long run by reducing waste, conserving energy, and making eco-conscious choices. This chapter division will provide practical tips on embracing a sustainable lifestyle without breaking the bank. From embracing minimalism to exploring eco-friendly alternatives, readers will gain insights into how sustainability can positively impact their financial freedom.

Overall, understanding the influence of lifestyle choices on financial independence is vital for individuals across various walks of life. By being mindful of our aesthetic preferences, evaluating our life choices, and adopting a sustainable lifestyle, we can make informed decisions that align with our financial goals. It aims to inspire spouses and professionals to make conscious choices that not only enhance their quality of life but also pave the way towards long-term financial freedom.

CHAPTER 3

CREATING A SUSTAINABLE LIFESTYLE FOR FINANCIAL INDEPENDENCE

Assessing Current Financial Situation and Setting Goals

In order to achieve financial freedom and build a sustainable life together, it is crucial for ProsumEducators to assess their current financial situation and set clear goals. This particular bit will guide you through the process, providing valuable insights and practical tips tailored to the niches of aesthetics, life and money, sustainable lifestyle, and financial independence.

Assessing your current financial situation is the first step towards achieving financial freedom. Begin by thoroughly analyzing your income, expenses, and debts. Take note of your monthly income from all sources and categorize your expenses into fixed, variable, and discretionary. This will give you a clear picture of where your money is going and help identify areas for improvement.

Next, evaluate your debts, including credit card balances, student loans, and mortgages. Understanding your debt-to-income ratio will enable you to devise an effective plan for debt repayment and reduce financial stress. Additionally, consider your credit score as it plays a vital role in securing financial opportunities and favorable interest rates.

After assessing your current situation, it is time to set financial goals that align with your values and aspirations. Whether it is saving for a dream vacation, starting a business, or early retirement, setting SMART goals (specific, measurable, achievable, relevant, and time-bound) is essential. Break down your long-term goals into smaller milestones to keep yourself motivated and on track.

To achieve financial freedom and sustain a fulfilling lifestyle, it is important to prioritize a sustainable approach to money management. This includes adopting mindful spending habits, reducing waste, and investing in eco-friendly options. By aligning your financial decisions with your values of sustainability, you not only contribute to a healthier planet but also save money in the long run.

Lastly, it will address the concept of financial independence. Whether you are a strict or lenient spender understanding the importance of financial independence empowers you to make informed decisions about your money. It involves creating multiple income streams, building an emergency fund, and investing wisely. By taking control of your financial future, you can enjoy peace of mind and the freedom to pursue your passions.

So, assessing your current financial situation and setting goals are vital steps towards achieving financial freedom and building a sustainable life together. By understanding your income, expenses, and debts and setting SMART goals, you can make informed decisions and work towards a secure financial future. Additionally, adopting a sustainable lifestyle and striving for financial independence will not only benefit you but also contribute to a better world.

Budgeting and Managing Expenses as a Couple

One of the key factors in building a sustainable life together as a couple is effectively managing your finances. In the following section, we will explore the topic of budgeting and managing expenses as a couple, providing valuable insights and practical tips to help you achieve financial freedom.

Budgeting is the foundation of any successful financial plan. It allows you to allocate your income towards essential expenses, savings, and discretionary spending. As a couple, it is crucial to create a joint budget that reflects both of your financial goals and priorities. This will ensure transparency, open communication, and alignment in your financial decisions.

To begin, start by identifying your combined income and fixed expenses such as rent or mortgage payments, utilities, insurance, and debt repayments. Then, allocate a portion of your income towards savings and investments. By prioritizing savings, you are building a safety net for unforeseen circumstances and setting the stage for future financial independence.

Next, tackle your variable expenses such as groceries, entertainment, and dining out. This is an opportunity to discuss and agree on spending limits in each category. Consider using budgeting apps or spreadsheets to track your expenses and monitor your progress.

Open and honest communication is essential when managing expenses as a couple. Regularly schedule money dates to discuss your financial goals, review your budget, and make adjustments if necessary. This will foster a sense of teamwork and ensure that both partners are actively involved in financial decision-making.

Another important aspect of managing expenses as a couple is finding ways to cut costs and live a more sustainable lifestyle. Explore ways to reduce your energy consumption, minimize waste, and opt for eco-friendly alternatives. Not only will this benefit the environment, but it can also save you money in the long run.

Furthermore, consider adopting a minimalist approach to consumption. By focusing on quality over quantity and avoiding unnecessary purchases, you can prioritize experiences and cultivate a more fulfilling life.

To sum up, budgeting and managing expenses as a couple is a vital step towards financial freedom and a sustainable lifestyle. By creating a joint budget, communicating openly, and making conscious choices, you can build a solid foundation for a prosperous future together. Remember, financial independence is not just about money; it is about aligning your life and money goals to create a harmonious and fulfilling life as a couple.

CHAPTER 4

INVESTING IN YOUR FUTURE

Introduction to Different Investment Options for Spouses in India

Investing is a crucial aspect of building a sustainable life together as spouses. It not only helps secure your financial future but also provides a means to achieve financial independence and a sustainable lifestyle. In India, there are various investment options available that cater to the diverse needs and goals of individuals. The objective of this chapter is to introduce you to some of these investment options, empowering you to make informed decisions about your financial future.

1. **Fixed Deposits (FDs):** FDs are a popular investment choice as they offer a fixed rate of interest over a specified period. They provide stability and security, making them ideal for risk-averse spouses. FDs are offered by banks and post offices, and the interest earned is taxable.
2. **Mutual Funds:** Mutual funds pool money from multiple investors to invest in a diversified portfolio of stocks, bonds, or other assets. They offer professional management and the potential for higher returns. As a spouse, you can choose from equity funds, debt funds, or hybrid funds based on your risk appetite and investment goals.

3. **Public Provident Fund (PPF):** PPF is a government-backed savings scheme that offers attractive interest rates and tax benefits. It has a lock-in period of 15 years, making it suitable for long-term financial goals such as retirement planning.

4. **Real Estate:** Investing in real estate can provide both rental income and capital appreciation. You can consider buying residential or commercial properties based on your financial capabilities and investment objectives. However, it is essential to conduct thorough research and understand the real estate market before making any investment decisions.

5. **Gold:** Gold has always been a preferred investment option in India. You can invest in physical gold, gold ETFs, or sovereign gold bonds. Gold acts as a hedge against inflation and currency fluctuations, making it a reliable long-term investment option.

6. **Stock Market:** Investing in stocks allows you to become a shareholder in a company and benefit from its growth. However, stock market investments come with risks, and it is crucial to have a good understanding of the market and conduct thorough research before investing.

Remember, each investment option has its own set of risks and rewards. It is essential to align your investment choices with your financial goals, risk tolerance, and time horizon. By diversifying your portfolio and regularly reviewing your investments, you can work towards achieving financial freedom and building a sustainable life together as spouses.

The aim is to provide you with a brief introduction to various investment options available in India. In the following chapters, we will delve deeper into each option, providing you with a comprehensive understanding and practical guidance to make informed investment decisions.

Risk Management and Diversification in the Indian Scenario

In today's volatile and uncertain economic landscape, it is imperative for individuals to understand the importance of risk management and diversification in order to achieve financial independence. This holds true for everyone, regardless of their roles in the society. By mastering these concepts, individuals can pave the way towards a sustainable lifestyle and financial freedom.

India, being one of the fastest-growing economies in the world, offers numerous opportunities for financial growth. However, it also comes with its fair share of risks and challenges. Therefore, it becomes crucial for individuals to develop a robust risk management strategy to safeguard their financial well-being.

One of the key aspects of risk management is diversification. By diversifying one's investments across various asset classes and sectors, individuals can mitigate the risk associated with a single investment. This strategy helps in reducing the impact of potential losses and maximizing returns. For instance, instead of investing all their savings in a single stock, individuals are advised to diversify their portfolio by including stocks from different sectors, bonds, real estate, or even alternative investment options like mutual funds and exchange-traded funds (ETFs).

Furthermore, risk management also involves assessing and managing risks associated with debt, insurance, and unforeseen events. It is essential to evaluate the risk appetite and have a contingency plan in place to tackle any untoward incidents that may impact one's financial stability. Adequate insurance coverage, emergency funds, and a well-structured debt management plan are vital components of a comprehensive risk management strategy.

In the Indian context, where cultural values often emphasize the importance of aesthetics, it is crucial to strike a balance between aesthetics, life, and money. While it is essential to enjoy life and pursue aesthetic aspirations, it is equally important to ensure financial stability and independence. This can be achieved by embracing a sustainable lifestyle that aligns with long-term financial goals and values.

Financial freedom for Partner Prospects can only be achieved through a holistic approach that encompasses risk management, diversification, and a commitment to sustainable living. By understanding the nuances of the Indian financial landscape, individuals can make informed decisions, protect their wealth, and build a sustainable life together.

CHAPTER 5

BUILDING MULTIPLE STREAMS OF INCOME

Exploring Side Hustles and Freelancing Opportunities

In today's fast-paced world, more and more individuals are seeking ways to supplement their income and achieve financial independence. Whether you are role fusionists or lifelong navigators, exploring side hustles and freelancing opportunities can be a game-changer in your quest for financial freedom. This piece, "Financial Freedom for Spouses: Building a Sustainable Life Together," will delve into the world of side hustles and freelancing, offering valuable insights and practical advice to help you embark on this exciting journey.

The Aesthetics niche encompasses various creative fields such as art, design, and fashion. For those with a passion for aesthetics, freelancing as a graphic designer, fashion consultant, or interior decorator can be a fulfilling way to earn an income. We will explore the different avenues available in this niche and provide guidance on how to market your skills and establish a solid client base.

Life and Money! These two aspects often intertwine, and understanding how to balance them is crucial. We will discuss side hustle opportunities in the wellness industry, including becoming a yoga instructor, personal trainer, or nutrition consultant. By exploring these avenues, you can not only earn a supplementary income but also contribute to a healthier and more sustainable lifestyle for yourself and others.

A sustainable lifestyle and financial independence go hand in hand. Within this subsection, we will explore into the world of eco-friendly side hustles and freelancing opportunities. From promoting green products and services to offering sustainable living consultations, there are numerous ways to align your passion for the environment with your financial goals. We will provide practical tips on how to establish yourself in this niche and attract clients who share your commitment to sustainability.

Financial freedom is not limited to a specific demographic. Whether you are a spouse looking to contribute to your household income, a professional seeking additional revenue streams, a student looking to fund your studies, or a consumer in search of financial independence, exploring side hustles and freelancing opportunities can be a stepping stone toward achieving your goals.

By exploring the various options available in aesthetics, life, and money! and sustainable lifestyle niches, you can find a side hustle or freelancing opportunity that aligns with your interests and values. This section will provide you with the knowledge and tools to embark on this exciting journey, empowering you to build a sustainable life together with your loved ones while achieving financial freedom.

Leveraging Skills and Talents for Additional Income

In today's world, where financial stability and independence are highly valued, it has become increasingly important for individuals, especially spouses, to explore different avenues to generate additional income. Fortunately, the modern age presents countless opportunities to leverage skills and talents to achieve financial freedom. Its proto-guides Engage Learners on how to tap into their unique abilities and interests to build a sustainable life together.

The connection between aesthetics, life, and money forms the foundation of this discussion. Many individuals possess skills or talents related to aesthetics, such as painting, photography, graphic design, or interior decoration. These talents can be transformed into profitable ventures, providing an additional income stream. By leveraging their creative abilities, individuals can offer their services in various industries, including advertising, event planning, or even starting their own businesses. This not only allows spouses to pursue their passions but also brings them closer to achieving financial independence.

Furthermore, adopting a sustainable lifestyle can also contribute to financial freedom. In recent years, the demand for eco-friendly and ethical products and services has soared. If you have an interest in sustainable living, you can explore opportunities to promote and sell environmentally friendly products, such as organic skincare or sustainable fashion. Additionally, you can share your knowledge and expertise through workshops or consultancy services, helping others lead a more sustainable lifestyle while generating income for yourself.

Another valuable aspect which should be discussed is empowering professionals and students to monetize their existing skills. With the rise of the gig economy, individuals can offer their expertise as freelancers or consultants in their respective fields. Whether you are a writer, graphic designer, programmer, or marketing specialist, there is a vast market for your skills online. By freelancing, professionals and students can utilize their abilities to earn additional income, gain valuable experience, and expand their professional network.

Ultimately, this subsection emphasizes the importance of recognizing one's unique talents and skills as valuable assets. It encourages growing individuals to explore avenues that align with their interests and passions, allowing them to generate additional income and work toward financial freedom. By leveraging these skills effectively, individuals can build a sustainable life together, achieving both personal fulfillment and financial independence.

CHAPTER 6

MANAGING DEBT AND CREDIT

Understanding Debt Repayment Strategies for Spouses

Debt is a common concern that many couples face in their journey towards financial freedom. It can cause stress, strain relationships, and hinder the ability to achieve long-term goals. However, by understanding and implementing effective debt repayment strategies, spouses can take control of their finances and build a sustainable life together. Within this section, we will explore various approaches that can help couples navigate the complexities of debt repayment.

First and foremost, spouses must have open and honest communication about their financial situation. This includes sharing information about debts, income, and expenses. By having a clear understanding of the overall picture, couples can work together to create a debt repayment plan that suits their unique circumstances. This plan should outline the specific debts, interest rates, and payment schedules.

One popular debt repayment strategy is the snowball method. This approach involves paying off the smallest debts first while making minimum payments on larger debts. As each small debt is eliminated, the extra money can be redirected towards larger debts, creating a sense of momentum and motivation. Another strategy is the avalanche method, which focuses on paying off debts with the highest interest rates first. This approach can save couples a significant amount of money in interest payments over time.

Consolidating debts is another option to consider. By combining multiple debts into a single loan with a lower interest rate, spouses can simplify their repayment process and potentially save money. However, it is important to carefully evaluate the terms and conditions of any consolidation offer to ensure it is truly beneficial in the long run.

Additionally, creating a realistic budget is essential for successful debt repayment. Spouses should track their income and expenses, identifying areas where they can cut back or make adjustments. By allocating a portion of their income towards debt repayment each month, couples can steadily reduce their debts while still maintaining a sustainable lifestyle.

Lastly, seeking professional advice can be invaluable for spouses navigating their debt repayment journey. Financial advisors like Chartered Accountants or even teachers and parents alike can provide personalized guidance based on individual circumstances, helping couples make informed decisions and develop effective strategies.

In conclusion, understanding and implementing debt repayment strategies are crucial for spouses seeking financial freedom and a sustainable life together. By openly communicating, exploring different approaches, creating budgets, and seeking professional advice, couples can take control of their debts and work towards a future of financial independence.

Building a Healthy Credit Score as a Couple

In today's society, a healthy credit score is essential for financial stability and independence. As a couple, it is important to understand the significance of maintaining a good credit score and how it can impact your financial goals and aspirations. This bit aims to provide you with valuable insights and strategies to build a healthy credit score as a couple, ensuring that you are well-prepared for a sustainable life together.

Primarily, it is crucial to have open and honest communication about your individual credit histories and scores. By sharing this information, you can identify any potential red flags or areas of improvement. Together, you can set financial goals and work towards improving your credit scores collectively.

One of the first steps in building a healthy credit score is to establish a budget and stick to it. By creating a realistic spending plan, you can ensure that you are making timely payments towards your debts and avoiding unnecessary expenses. This will reflect positively on your credit report and contribute to a higher credit score.

Another vital aspect of building a healthy credit score is to make all payments on time. This includes credit card bills, loan installments, and any other financial obligations. Late payments can negatively affect your credit score and may hinder your ability to secure loans or obtain favorable interest rates in the Future. By being diligent with payment deadlines, you can establish a reputation as a responsible borrower.

Furthermore, it is important to minimize your debt-to-credit ratio. This ratio compares the amount of debt you have to your available credit limit. Maintaining a low ratio demonstrates financial discipline and responsibility. As a couple, you can work together to pay off existing debts and avoid accumulating unnecessary credit card balances.

Lastly, regularly monitoring your credit reports is imperative. By checking your reports for any errors or discrepancies, you can address them promptly and ensure that your credit score accurately reflects your financial health. There are various online platforms that offer free credit reports, making it easier than ever to stay on top of your credit profile.

By implementing these strategies and building a healthy credit score as a couple, you are laying the foundation for a sustainable lifestyle and financial independence. A solid credit score will provide you with greater opportunities and flexibility in achieving your shared goals and aspirations. Remember, it takes teamwork and commitment to maintain a healthy credit score, but the rewards are well worth the effort.

CHAPTER 7

SAVING FOR SHORT-TERM AND LONG- TERM GOALS

Strategies for Building an Emergency Fund

In today's uncertain world, having a robust emergency fund is essential for financial stability and peace of mind. Whether you are a professional or a student, understanding the strategies for building an emergency fund can help you navigate unexpected financial challenges and work towards a sustainable and independent lifestyle. In this topic, we will explore effective strategies that can assist you in building a solid emergency fund.

1. **Start Small and Be Consistent:** Begin by setting achievable goals. Saving a small amount each month consistently is far more effective than sporadically saving large sums. Aim to save at least 10% of your income and gradually increase it as your financial situation improves.

2. **Create a Budget:** Developing a realistic budget is crucial for identifying areas where you can cut back on unnecessary expenses. By tracking your income and expenditures, you can redirect funds toward your emergency fund.

3. **Automate Savings:** Take advantage of automation tools offered by banks and financial institutions. Set up a recurring transfer from your checking account to a

separate savings account dedicated solely to your emergency fund. This way, you won't have to rely on willpower to save consistently.

4. **Minimize Debt:** High-interest debts can drain your finances and hinder your ability to save. Prioritize paying down debts, starting with those with the highest interest rates. By reducing debt, you'll free up more funds to contribute to your emergency fund.
5. **Increase Your Income:** Consider exploring side hustles or part-time jobs to supplement your primary source of income. The additional income can be directly channeled into your emergency fund, helping you build it faster.
6. **Cut Back on Non-Essential Expenses:** Evaluate your spending habits and identify areas where you can cut back. For example, eating out less frequently, reducing entertainment expenses, or finding more affordable alternatives for your hobbies.
7. **Set Realistic Expectations:** Building an emergency fund takes time and discipline. It's important to set realistic expectations and not get discouraged along the way. Remember, every rupee saved brings you closer to financial freedom and security.

By implementing these strategies, you'll be on your way to building a robust emergency fund. Whether you're aiming for a sustainable lifestyle, financial independence, or simply seeking peace of mind, having a solid emergency fund will provide you with the necessary buffer to navigate unexpected financial storms. Start today, and take control of your financial future!

Early Habit of Small and Big Savings - Money Market and Capital Market

Introduction: In order to achieve financial freedom and build a sustainable life together, it is imperative to develop healthy saving habits from an early stage.

Whether you are a holistic player or focused individual, understanding the concepts of the money and capital markets can play a crucial role in your journey toward financial independence. Now, we will look into the importance of small and big savings and how the money and capital markets can help you grow your wealth.

1. **The Power of Small Savings:** Small savings may seem insignificant, but they can make a significant impact on your financial well-being. By cultivating the habit of saving even a small portion of your income, you can gradually build a substantial nest egg. In this section, we will explore the practical tips and techniques to save money, including budgeting, automating savings, and cutting unnecessary expenses. By making small sacrifices today, you can reap the rewards of financial freedom tomorrow.

2. **Understanding the Money Market:** The money market is a segment of the financial market where short-term borrowing and lending of funds take place. It offers opportunities to invest in low-risk and highly liquid instruments such as treasury bills, commercial papers, and Certificates of deposit. This division will explain the benefits of money market investments, their potential returns, and how you can leverage them to grow your savings.

3. **Exploring the Capital Market:** The capital market, on the other hand, deals with long-term investments in stocks, bonds, and mutual funds. This market provides opportunities to earn higher returns but also carries higher risks. Here, we will study the basics of capital market

investments, including the understanding of stock markets, bonds, and diversification strategies. It will also emphasize the importance of seeking professional advice and conducting thorough research before venturing into the capital market.

4. **Building a Sustainable Lifestyle:** Financial independence goes hand in hand with sustainable living. In this part of the chapter, we will examine methods to align your lifestyle choices with your financial goals. It will discuss the importance of conscious consumption, ethical investing, and making environmentally-friendly choices. By adopting a sustainable lifestyle, you not only contribute to a better future but also create a solid foundation for your financial well-being.

Conclusion: Developing early habits of small and big savings, along with a deep understanding of the money market and capital market, can pave the way for financial freedom. By embracing sustainable practices and making informed investment decisions, you can build a life that is aesthetically pleasing, financially secure, and aligned with your values. Start your journey today and unlock the path to a sustainable lifestyle and financial independence.

Planning for Retirement and Future Expenses

Retirement is a phase of life that everyone looks forward to, as it offers the opportunity to relax, pursue hobbies, and spend quality time with loved ones. However, without proper planning, retirement can quickly turn into a financial nightmare. Here, we will look into the importance of planning for retirement and future expenses and provide you with valuable insights on how to achieve financial freedom and a sustainable lifestyle.

Understanding the significance of retirement planning is crucial for the common man. It is never too early to start saving for retirement, as the power of compounding can work wonders over time. By setting aside a portion of your income each month, you can build a substantial nest egg that will support you during your golden years.

One key aspect of planning for retirement is determining your future expenses. Analyze your current lifestyle and anticipate any major expenses that may arise in the future, such as healthcare costs, travel plans, or home renovations. This exercise will help you estimate the amount of money you will need for a comfortable retirement and allow you to set realistic savings goals.

To achieve financial independence and a sustainable lifestyle, it is essential to adopt a long-term mindset. Make wise and sound investment decisions, diversify your portfolio, and take advantage of tax-efficient retirement savings accounts. Educate yourself about different investment options and seek professional advice if needed. Remember, the more informed you are, the better equipped you will be to make sound financial decisions.

Additionally, it is crucial to stay disciplined and avoid unnecessary expenses. Prioritize your financial goals and resist the temptation to overspend on non-essential items. By adopting a frugal mindset, you can maximize your savings and accelerate your journey towards financial freedom.

Lastly, regularly reassess your retirement plan and adjust it as necessary. Life is unpredictable, and circumstances may change. Periodically review your investments, evaluate your progress, and make any necessary adjustments to ensure that your retirement goals remain on track.

In conclusion, planning for retirement and future expenses is a vital component of achieving financial freedom and a sustainable lifestyle. By starting early, setting realistic goals, making informed investment decisions, and staying disciplined, you can secure a comfortable retirement and enjoy the fruits of your labor. Remember, it is never too late to take control of your financial future and build a life that balances aesthetics, life, and money, and promotes sustainable living.

CHAPTER 8

NAVIGATING FINANCIAL CHALLENGES AS A COUPLE

Dealing with Financial Disagreements and Conflict

Money matters can be a significant source of tension in any relationship. Financial disagreements can arise due to differences in spending habits, priorities, and financial goals. However, understanding how to navigate these conflicts is crucial for maintaining a healthy and sustainable relationship. Now, we will explore the effective strategies for dealing with financial disagreements and conflicts, promoting financial freedom and a harmonious partnership.

1. **Communication is key:** Open and honest communication is vital when it comes to discussing finances. Spouses need to create a safe space where they can express their concerns, goals, and fears about money. By actively listening to each other's perspectives, couples can develop a deeper understanding of their financial attitudes and work towards finding common ground.

2. **Set shared financial goals:** Building a sustainable life together requires setting shared financial goals. Define short-term and long-term objectives that align with your aspirations as a couple. By establishing common targets, you can work as a team, supporting each other's efforts

and reducing conflicts that may arise due to differing priorities.

3. **Create a budget together:** A budget serves as a roadmap for financial decision-making. Involve both partners in creating a budget that reflects their values and priorities. Regularly review and revise the budget as circumstances change. This collaborative approach ensures that both spouses have a say in financial matters, reducing the potential for conflicts.
4. **Seek professional help if needed:** Sometimes, financial disagreements can become overwhelming, affecting the overall well-being of the relationship. In such cases, it may be beneficial to seek assistance from a financial advisor or a marriage counselor who specializes in financial matters. These professionals can provide objective insights and strategies to help resolve conflicts and create a sustainable financial plan.
5. **Compromise and find common ground:** Financial conflicts can often be resolved through compromise. Evaluate each other's financial concerns and find ways to meet halfway. This may involve adjusting spending habits, finding alternative solutions, or seeking out opportunities for additional income. By working together to find common ground, couples can achieve financial independence while nurturing a harmonious relationship.

By implementing these strategies, spouses can effectively navigate financial disagreements and conflicts, fostering a sustainable lifestyle and financial independence. Remember, financial freedom is not just about the numbers; it is about building a strong and resilient partnership that supports the overall well-being of both individuals.

Overcoming Common Financial Roadblocks

In our journey towards financial freedom, we often encounter various roadblocks that hinder our progress. These roadblocks can range from personal habits to external factors, but they can be overcome with the right mindset and strategies.

One common financial roadblock is overspending. Many of us fall into the trap of living beyond their means, accumulating debt, and struggling to make ends meet. To overcome this roadblock, it is crucial to develop a budget and stick to it. By tracking expenses and distinguishing between needs and wants, individuals can regain control over their finances and start saving for a sustainable future.

Another roadblock that prevents us from achieving financial independence is the lack of financial literacy. Many people, despite their education and professional achievements, lack the necessary knowledge about personal finance. This is especially true for individuals in the niches of aesthetics, life and money, sustainable lifestyle, and financial independence. To overcome this roadblock, it is essential to invest time and effort in educating ourselves about money management, investing, and building wealth. There are numerous resources available, including books, online courses, and financial advisors, which can provide valuable insights and guidance.

One significant roadblock that affects spouses is the lack of communication and shared financial goals. Many couples struggle to align their financial priorities and make joint decisions about money. To overcome this roadblock, it is crucial for spouses to have open and honest conversations about their financial aspirations, fears, and expectations. By setting common goals and working together towards them, couples can build a sustainable life together and achieve financial freedom.

External factors, such as economic downturns or unexpected expenses, can also pose challenges on our path to financial freedom. While we cannot always control these events, we can prepare for them. By building an emergency fund and having adequate insurance coverage, individuals can protect themselves from unforeseen circumstances and ensure their financial stability.

Overcoming common financial roadblocks requires commitment, discipline, and a willingness to learn and adapt. By addressing our spending habits, improving our financial literacy, fostering communication and shared goals with our partners, and preparing for unexpected events, we can overcome these roadblocks and pave the way toward a sustainable and financially independent future.

CHAPTER 9

TEACHING FINANCIAL LITERACY TO CHILDREN AND FUTURE GENERATIONS

Instilling Money Values and Habits in Your Children: Indian vis a vis Western Countries

When it comes to teaching children about money, each culture has its unique approach. Discover the differences in money values and habits between Indian and Western countries and learn how to incorporate the best practices from both cultures to raise financially responsible children. Together, we can work towards building a brighter and more financially stable future for ourselves and future generations.

In Indian culture, financial literacy is highly valued and often begins at an early age. Parents in India emphasize the importance of saving money, investing wisely, and practicing frugality. Children are taught to differentiate between needs and wants, and the value of hard work is instilled through chores and responsibilities.

On the other hand, Western countries tend to focus more on financial independence and entrepreneurship. Children are encouraged to take risks, think creatively, and develop their own businesses from a young age.

The concept of financial freedom and generating wealth is deeply ingrained in Western societies.

To effectively instill money values and habits in your children, it is essential to strike a balance between these two approaches. Teach your children the importance of saving money, budgeting, and living within their means, drawing inspiration from the Indian culture. Encourage them to work towards financial independence and explore entrepreneurial opportunities, taking cues from the Western mindset.

Introduce your children to the concept of sustainable lifestyle and financial independence, which resonates with the niches of aesthetics, life, and money. Teach them about ethical investing, responsible consumption, and the impact of their financial decisions on the environment and society. By combining the best practices from both cultures, you can raise financially responsible children who are conscious of their impact on the world.

As prosumer learners, it is crucial to lead by example and incorporate these money values and habits into your own lives. Practice open communication about money matters within your family, set financial goals together, and encourage your children to contribute to the family's financial decisions. By involving them in discussions about budgeting, saving, and investing, you will empower them to make informed choices and develop a healthy relationship with money.

In conclusion, understanding the differences in money values and habits between Indian and Western cultures allows us to adopt the best practices from both. By instilling these values in our children and leading by example, we can pave the way for a financially independent and sustainable future.

Planning for Their Financial Future

In today's fast-paced world, it is crucial for couples to plan for their financial future. Whether you are newlyweds just starting your life together or have been married for years, taking control of your finances is essential for building a sustainable life together. This bit aims to guide us in understanding the importance of financial planning and how it can lead to a sustainable lifestyle and financial independence.

Financial planning is not just about budgeting and saving; it is a comprehensive approach to managing your money and making informed decisions about your future. It involves setting financial goals, creating a budget, managing debt, investing wisely, and protecting your assets. By planning for the future, couples can achieve financial stability, reduce stress, and build a solid foundation for their life together.

One of the first steps in planning for your financial future is to set clear financial goals. These goals can be short-term, such as saving for a vacation or paying off debt, or long-term, such as buying a house or planning for retirement. By identifying your goals, you can create a roadmap to guide your financial decisions and prioritize your spending.

Creating a budget is another crucial aspect of financial planning. A budget helps you track your income and expenses, ensuring that you are living within your means. It allows you to allocate funds for your goals, pay off debt, and save for emergencies or future expenses. By following a budget, couples can avoid unnecessary debt and build a solid financial foundation.

Managing debt is also an important part of planning for your financial future. High-interest debts, such as credit card debt or student loans, can hinder your ability to save and invest. By creating a plan to pay off debt strategically, couples can free up more money to save and invest, thereby accelerating their path to financial independence.

Investing wisely is another key aspect of planning for the future. Investing allows your money to grow over time, providing you with a nest egg for retirement or other long-term goals. Understanding the basics of investing, such as diversification and risk management, can help you make informed decisions and maximize your returns.

Lastly, protecting your assets is essential for financial security. This includes having appropriate insurance coverage, such as health insurance, life insurance, and property insurance. By protecting yourself and your assets, you can safeguard against unexpected events and ensure that your financial future remains secure.

In summary, planning for your financial future is essential for building a sustainable life together. By setting clear financial goals, creating a budget, managing debt, investing wisely, and protecting your assets, couples can achieve financial stability and independence. The objective of this subsection is to provide life spectrals with the tools and knowledge to plan for a secure and prosperous future.

CHAPTER 10

THRIVING AS FINANCIALLY INDEPENDENT SPOUSES

Celebrating Successes and Milestones Along the Way

In our journey towards financial freedom, it is important to pause and acknowledge the successes and milestones we achieve along the way.

As a life role synthesist, this ultimate topic of "Celebrating Successes and Milestones Along the Way" is designed to inspire and motivate you to continue on your path towards building a sustainable life together.

One of the key aspects of celebrating successes is recognizing the progress we make in our financial journey. This can be as simple as paying off a credit card debt, saving a certain amount of money each month, or achieving a milestone in our long-term financial goals. By acknowledging these accomplishments, we create a positive mindset and boost our motivation to keep going.

As spouses, celebrating successes together can strengthen your bond and create a sense of unity in your financial goals. By setting shared milestones and rewarding yourselves when you achieve them, you create a supportive and encouraging environment that will propel you both towards financial independence. This could be as extravagant as planning a special trip or as simple as enjoying a date night at home.

Professionals and students can also benefit from celebrating their financial successes. Whether it's receiving a promotion, earning a higher salary, or graduating debt-free, these achievements should not go unnoticed. By acknowledging these milestones, you reinforce your belief in your ability to manage your finances effectively, leading to even greater success in the future.

For consumers, celebrating successes can be as simple as resisting the temptation to make impulsive purchases or sticking to a budget for a certain period of time. By rewarding yourself with a small treat or a night out, you reinforce positive financial behavior and create a pattern of responsible spending.

Regardless of your niche, whether it's aesthetics, life and money, sustainable lifestyle, or financial independence, celebrating successes and milestones is an essential part of your journey. It not only provides motivation and encouragement but also serves as a reminder of your progress and the impact your efforts have on your financial well-being.

In conclusion, a huge emphasis is placed on the importance of recognizing and celebrating achievements in our pursuit of financial freedom. By acknowledging these successes, we create a positive mindset, strengthen relationships, and reinforce our commitment to building a sustainable life together. So, let us pause, celebrate, and continue on our path toward financial independence with renewed determination and enthusiasm.

Sustaining a Balanced and Fulfilling Life Together - Social, Political, Financial, Creative and Sustainable Growth

In today's fast-paced world, finding a balance between our social, political, financial, creative, and sustainable growth can often seem like an overwhelming task. However, it is crucial for us to understand that achieving this balance is not only possible but also vital for building a sustainable life together. This bit will explore the various aspects of sustaining a balanced and fulfilling life, focusing on the niches of aesthetics, life and money, sustainable lifestyle, and financial independence.

When it comes to aesthetics, we often tend to focus on external beauty and overlook the importance of inner harmony. In this section, we will delve into the concept of holistic beauty, emphasizing the significance of self-care, mindfulness, and cultivating positive relationships. By nurturing our inner beauty, we can enhance our overall well-being and contribute positively to our relationships and communities.

Life and money are deeply interconnected, and achieving financial freedom is a goal shared by many. This part will provide practical tips and strategies for managing finances as a couple, discussing topics such as budgeting, saving, investing, and debt management. By adopting smart financial habits and open communication, spouses can work towards a more secure and prosperous future.

A sustainable lifestyle is an increasingly prevalent topic in our society, as more people recognize the importance of preserving the environment for future generations. Through this section, we will explore ways to incorporate sustainable practices into our daily lives, such as reducing waste, conserving energy, and supporting eco-friendly businesses. By collectively embracing sustainability, we can make a significant impact on our planet and inspire others to join the cause.

Finally, we will examine the concept of financial independence, which goes beyond merely accumulating wealth. True financial independence means having the freedom to pursue our passions, engage in creative endeavors, and contribute meaningfully to society. This section will provide insights on leveraging our skills and resources to create fulfilling careers, businesses, and philanthropic initiatives.

In conclusion, sustaining a balanced and fulfilling life together requires a holistic approach that encompasses social, political, financial, creative, and sustainable growth. By actively engaging in these areas, role fusionists can establish a harmonious existence that not only benefits themselves but also contributes positively to the world around them. By embracing aesthetics, life and money, sustainable lifestyle, and financial independence, we can build a sustainable life together that is both personally and globally transformative.

Worksheets and Templates for Budgeting and Goal Setting

In our journey towards financial freedom, one of the most crucial steps is to establish a solid budget and set clear goals.

Managing money effectively not only brings stability and security to our lives but also paves the way for a sustainable lifestyle and financial independence. To assist you in this process, we have compiled a collection of worksheets and templates that will guide you in creating a realistic budget and setting achievable goals.

1. **Budgeting Worksheets:** Budgeting is the foundation of financial success. These worksheets are designed to help you analyze your income, expenses, and savings. By tracking your spending habits, you can identify areas where you can cut back and save more effectively. Our worksheets will empower you to create a personalized budget that aligns with your financial goals and values.

2. **Goal Setting Templates:** Setting goals gives you a clear direction and purpose. These templates will assist you in defining short-term and long-term financial objectives. Whether you aim to pay off debts, save for a down payment on a house, or invest for retirement, these templates will help you map out the steps needed to achieve your aspirations. By breaking down goals into

manageable tasks, you can stay motivated and track your progress.

3. **Aesthetic Budgeting:** We understand that aesthetics play a significant role in our lives. Our aesthetically designed worksheets and templates combine functionality with visual appeal, making the budgeting and goal-setting process enjoyable. We believe that when you appreciate the tools you use, you are more likely to engage with them regularly, leading to greater success in managing your finances.

4. **Life and Money:** This bit delves into the intricate relationship between life and money. We explore how aligning your spending habits with your values can create a fulfilling and purpose-driven life. The worksheets and templates provided will guide you in reflecting on your priorities and making intentional financial decisions that support your desired lifestyle.

5. **Sustainable Lifestyle and Financial Independence:** Building a sustainable life together goes beyond budgeting; it encompasses conscious consumption, environmental responsibility, and financial independence. Our worksheets and templates will help you evaluate your environmental impact and develop sustainable spending habits.

Additionally, we offer guidance on building wealth, reducing debt, and achieving financial independence, empowering you to live the life you desire while safeguarding the planet for future generations.

By utilizing these worksheets and templates, you will gain the tools necessary to take control of your finances, build a sustainable life, and achieve financial independence. Start your journey towards financial freedom today!